Michael Bhim

Tuesday

T0347883

Bloomsbury Methuen Drama
An imprint of Bloomsbury Publishing Plc

B L O O M S B U R Y
LONDON · OXFORD · NEW YORK · NEW DELHI · SYDNEY

Bloomsbury Methuen Drama

An imprint of Bloomsbury Publishing Plc

Imprint previously known as Methuen Drama

50 Bedford Square	1385 Broadway
London	New York
WC1B 3DP	NY 10018
UK	USA

www.bloomsbury.com

**BLOOMSBURY, METHUEN DRAMA and the Diana
logo are trademarks of Bloomsbury Publishing Plc**

First published 2016

© Michael Bhim, 2016

British Library Cataloguing-in-Publication Data
A catalogue record for this book is available from the British Library.

ISBN: PB: 978-1-3500-3052-7
ePDF: 978-1-3500-3051-0
ePub: 978-1-3500-3053-4

Library of Congress Cataloging-in-Publication Data
A catalog record for this book is available from the Library of Congress

Cover design: Adriana Brioso
Cover image © Al Smith

Typeset by Mark Heslington Ltd, Scarborough, North Yorkshire

The White Bear Theatre and Robert Wisepart present

TUESDAY

By **Michael Bhim**

TUESDAY was first performed at The White Bear Theatre
on Tuesday 18th October 2016

The White Bear Theatre wish to thank the following for their help with
this production: Patrick Marmion, The Tommyfield, John O'Donovan,
Naomi Ray @Studiopixie, Nick Quinn, The Staff at the White Bear,
Simon Usher, Dashti Jahfar, Neil Grutchfield.

TUESDAY

By Michael Bhim

Cast in order of appearance

Edward	**Thomas-Jan Johnston**
Brian	**Jermaine Dominique**
Nic	**Kate Burdette**
Linda	**Pheobe Ladenburg**

Director	**Michael Kingsbury**
Associate Director	**Lucy Curtis**
Designer	**Adelaide Green**
Lighting Designer	**Luke M Francis**
Composers	**The Mason Brothers**
Producer	**Robert Wisepart**
Literary Associates	**Georgia Harris, Cameron Cooke, David Cottis**

WRITER

Michael Bhim (Writer)

Michael Bhim is an award-winning playwright and screenwriter. His first play, *Distant Violence,* produced at the Tricycle Theatre, was nominated for the Meyer Whitworth Award. He is also winner of the Alfred Fagon Award. He has been produced at the Soho Theatre, Royal Court Theatre and Almeida. He has written for BBC Radio. For television he has written for the BBC (BBC/Leopard films), with work in development with Sky Television (Acme/Sky TV), Miramax (USA).

CAST

Thomas-Jan Johnston (Edward)

Thomas's credits include *Barred* for Stretch (UK tour); *Love on the Dole* directed by Lucy Curtis (Space Arts Centre), alongside playing Hortensio in *The Taming of Shrew* directed by Beth Vyse, and Kevin in *Port* by Simon Stephens, directed by Richard Pepper.

Jermaine Dominique (Brian)

His theatre work includes: *Macbeth* (Shakespeare's Globe Theatre); *Ma Rainey's Black Bottom* (National Theatre); *Repast 2, Asylum* and *Comming Home* (Theatre503); *Terms and Conditions* (White Bear); *Don Quixote – 21 Windmills for Bred in the Bone*, *The Making of Moo* (Orange Tree Theatre); *Little Sweet Thing* for Outreach; *The Taming of the Shrew* for No pigeon; *Hamlet* and *As You Like It* for Dark Cloud; and *The Island* (Rose Bruford directors production). Films include: *The Pugilist*, *Salvage* and *Turtle Eggs*. Radio includes: *Ealing*.

Kate Burdette (Nic)

Her theatre work includes: *66 Books* (The Bush); *Sweet Nothings* (The Young Vic); *Song of Deborah* at (The Lowry) and *The Man Outside* at the (Theatre Royal Haymarket). For film she played Allegra Betts in David Hare's *Worricker Trilogy*. She played Lady Harriett in *The Duchess*. Her TV credits include: *EastEnders*, *Silent Witness*, *The Dark Side of the Earth*.

Pheobe Ladenburg (Linda)

Phoebe trained at the Royal Central School of Speech and Drama where she was awarded the Embassy Scholarship and was nominated by the school for the Spotlight Graduate Prize. Theatre includes: *Gift Return* (Park Theatre); *Nine Weeks* (Arts Theatre) and *Doll* (Keble College Oxford). TV includes: *American Monster* (Discovery USA).

COMPANY

Michael Kingsbury (Director)

Theatre credits include the critically acclaimed *Ying Tong* (West Yorkshire Playhouse and subsequent transfer to the Ambassadors Theatre); *In Lambeth* (Southwark Playhouse); the London premiere of *States of Shock* (BAC); *This Other Eden* (Soho Theatre); *Seduced* (written and directed for Finborough Theatre); *The Divided Laing* (Arcola); *Doomsday* (Southwark Playhouse). His work at the Salisbury Playhouse includes Steven Berkoff's *Decadence* and new adaptations of *Hard Times* and *The Hound of the Baskervilles*. He directed the world premiere of *A Musical Homage to Radio 4* for the Watermill Theatre, Newbury, and ACT Productions, and is currently developing Jack Sherperd's play about Edvard Munch in association with the Royal Academy of Dramatic Art. His play *All Manner of Means* was Time Out Critics Choice at the BAC and subsequently transferred to the King's Head Theatre. Michael produced and directed the hugely successful *Round the Horne … Revisited*, which ran in the West End for over a year, completed three number one tours, was chosen for the Royal Variety Performance and subsequently adapted for BBC television. Michael has also directed numerous overseas tours with the British Council.

Lucy Curtis (Associate Director)

Lucy is the Artistic Director and co-founder of Changing Face, a multi-lingual, multi-national theatre company specialising in international drama and documentary theatre. Her credits in partnership with the company include: *Where Will We Live?* (Southwark Playhouse); *It Is So Ordered* (Oxford Playhouse); *Love on the Dole* (The Space); and *Clay* (Pleasance). Her previous credits include: *Women's Stories of Ford Dagenham* (Queen's Theatre Hornchurch) and *The Divided Laing* (Arcola). She is currently developing productions with the Albany, Deptford and a co-production with the Arcola.

Robert Wisepart (Producer)

After training at the London School of Dramatic Art, Robert's first professional job was with the Folkstone Repertory Company. While he was there, he managed to break into films, playing Frank Sinatra's son in *The Naked Runner*. His other film credits include the Mike Sarne film *Joanna* with Donald Sutherland; *Yanks* with Richard Gere; *Cromwell* with Richard Harris and Alec Guinness, and *Goodbye, Mr Chips* with Peter O'Toole and Petula Clark. Other credits include: *My Giddy Aunt* at the Savoy Theatre, West End and UK tour; and *A Bridge Too Far* with Robert Redford, Laurence Olivier, directed by Richard Attenborough.

Robert's producing credits include: *The Guessing Game* at the Yvonne Arnaud Theatre Guildford and UK tour; *The Other Side of the Room*, UK tour, and *Apartment 2012* at the White Bear Theatre directed by Michael Kingsbury.

Adelaide Green (Designer)

Adelaide studied stage management and technical theatre at the Academy of Live and Recorded Arts, specialising in design. She then went on to study theatre design at Wimbledon College of Art. Her theatre credits include: Costume Design: *You Can Still Make a Killing, A Midsummer Night's Dream* (ALRA Theatre); Costume and Set Design: *Alice, How Curious You Are . . .* (ALRA Theatre); Design Assistant: *Daisy Pulls It Off, Love and Information,* (ALRA Theatre); Costume Assistant: *Grimm Tales, Playhouse Creatures* (ALRA Theatre); Stagecraft Assistant: *Respect/Buy Nothing Day, Playhouse Creature, Love of a Nightingale* (ALRA Theatre).

Luke M. Francis (Lighting Designer)

Luke studied at the Academy of Live and Recorded Arts, where he specialised as an Assistant Lighting Designer and Chief Electrician.

While training at ALRA, he worked as a Duty Technician at the King's Head Theatre in Islington and since graduating in 2016, he works as a Lighting Technician at the Hampstead Theatre and the Southwark Playhouse.

The Mason Brothers (Composers)

Imogen and Ellie Mason are multi-instrumentalists and composers, best known for their work in experimental trio Wovoka Gentle. Their first foray into the world of theatre was creating soundscapes with avant-garde performance company Stasis at their 2014 Edinburgh production of *A Table*; which was swiftly followed by a commission to score the world premier of *What's Eating Gilbert Grape* (directed by Alex Howarth and co-adapted by Peter Hedges) in London later that year. They have since gone on to score three further plays for Alex Howarth's Patch of Blue theatre company, alongside a number of short films. Their compositions have enjoyed extended runs in London's West End, Edinburgh, Dubai and New York, with their latest work, *We Live By The Sea*, premiering in Adelaide in the new year.

The White Bear Theatre

The White Bear has a long-standing commitment to offering opportunities to emerging theatre-makers. We place a great deal of importance on involving playwrights in the process of production, encouraging their input and engagement throughout. This has proven to be a very rewarding approach for playwrights, offering a high degree of artistic control over their own work.

The White Bear re-launched in October 2016 as part of a major redevelopment of the building. This play leads the opening season of the brand new White Bear Theatre.

Transfers from the White Bear have included the recent production of *Inigo* transferring to The Pleasance, *The Confessions of Gordon Brown* and *Madness in Valencia* both for the Trafalgar 2, and *Round the Horne… Revisited* which played in the West End for eighteen months, completed three first-class tours and was chosen for the Royal Variety Performance. The London première of John Osborne's second play, *Personal Enemy*, transferred to the prestigious Brits Off-Broadway Festival in New York, and other transfers include *The Duchess of Malfi* to the Southwark Playhouse, and *Count Oederland* to the Arcola.

Michael Bhim joins an impressive list of theatre-makers who have worked with The White Bear, including Joe Penhall, Emily Watson, Tamzin Outhwaite, Kwame Kwei Armah, Vicky Featherstone, Torben Betts and Lucinda Coxon.

Artwork by @Studiopixie

Tuesday

For little Almie

Characters

Edward, *mid thirties*
Brian, *mid thirties*
Nic, *woman, early thirties*
Linda, *late thirties*

Setting

A small flat in Kilburn, North West London.

Note on text

Use of ellipsis express an unfinished thought, nervousness or being distracted by a memory.

Scene One

Edward's flat. Living room. **Edward** *and* **Brian** *sit, a coffee table with drinks between them. Early hours.*

Edward   Remember . . . ?

Brian   I'm . . . I can picture him . . . I can.

Edward   His name . . . come on.

Brian   Name. OK . . . Thoughts . . . thinking . . . Shit . . .

Edward   Baptiste!

Brian   Bap-fucking-tiste!

Edward   Yes!

Brian   Almost had it . . . Yes. I remember . . . Black guy.

Edward   Yes.

Brian   Six-two.

Edward   No.

Brian   No . . . ?

Edward   Taller . . . Way taller.

Brian   . . . Taller than us, yes . . . In assembly he'd always, always point out how thin I was on top. Remember that? Piece of shit . . .

Edward   Baptiste . . .

Slight pause.

Brian   Some would call him a cunt . . . Some . . . If . . . if it wasn't for his . . .

Edward   Always friendly . . . ?

Brian   Was a cunt but friendly. With everybody. (*Slight pause.*) Let me guess . . . Drug addict? A few from the Vaughan have gone that way. Catholics . . . we're the worst.

Edward   Asset manager.

Brian   Kidding me . . .

Edward   Coutts.

Brian   Fuck off! The Queen's fucking bank?

Edward   Looked him up on Linkedin.

Brian   There's no justice . . .

Slight pause.

Brian   Must be some assistant . . . Internet profiles . . .
Write what you want about yourself. Half of it untrue.

Edward   Don't know. Saw him in Hampstead. Sunday.

Brian   What is it with these wankers? Travel all the way
from Penge, some shit hole, to sit in Hampstead . . . With
some fucking notepad, dressing gown, slippers. Make
everyone think they're local . . . just soaking in the *ambience*
of their successful lives to write some *novel* . . .

Edward   . . . I was actually in Hampstead . . . with my
notepad . . . writing my novel. I don't live in Penge but . . .

Brian   That's different . . . Different, Eddie.

Edward   Was doing a bit of marking . . . on the side.

Brian   Yes . . . Like I said . . . Not you. . . . Other people.

Edward   I write a diary. But . . . diary of work, it helps me
. . . The students, so many of them.

Brian   Work is work, don't knock that, no way! But
these . . . *writers* . . . you know . . . ? (*Slight pause.*) Dated a
writer . . .

Edward   Really . . .?

Brian   Long time ago. She was depressed. Moody . . . Took
her out . . . Give her some inspiration . . . Couple movies.
Amsterdam . . . you know? Help her with her 'writing' . . .

Too prudish to watch a sex show . . . smoke a bit of hash. Aren't these people supposed to be the fucking shaman of the fucking village? Live the lives we're too fucking afraid to live? (*Slight pause.*) She never made it by the way. Didn't have what it took . . . Last time I looked her up . . . ? Writing for Gardeners' World . . .

Edward   Never dated a writer.

Brian   Good. Don't. The depression, highs, lows, weird sex . . . They write all day cos they're too afraid to live life . . . not like us.

Edward   Yep, not like us . . . You're not living you're dying. Who said that?

Long pause.

Edward   So Baptiste.

Brian   Yes . . . tell me . . .

Edward   He was . . .

Brian   Tell me everything . . .

Edward   I'm trying to . . .

Brian   Paint a picture. What did he have on . . . ?

Edward   . . . Had these . . . what is it . . . Alexander McQueen's on . . .

Brian   What?

Edward   Some shoes.

Brian   Fuck me . . . That's very fashion conscious, Ed . . . ? You know the names of his shoes?

Edward   No, only knew cos he made a point of saying . . . 'Look at my Alexander McQueen's' . . . Soft leather jacket, casual successful look.

Brian   Probably married to some not so attractive, deep-pocketed old bird in her 50s . . . Dress up their young boys like dolls . . . I see it all the time. No integrity . . . Grab hold

of these women, have a child or two . . . Anything to climb
the ladder.

Edward   Two kids, pretty mother . . . She looked younger
than us.

Brian   Great . . .

Edward   Pretty . . . Not just because she was blonde, but she
was actually, without the hair, her face. . . . I looked at her
face. I was jealous . . . Addicted to look at her. Some faces
have that quality . . .

Brian   Never my cup of tea, blondes . . . Brunettes . . .
Brazilians. Spanish. Something with a bit of a tan . . .

Edward   Noticed him from the top of one of the roads that
cuts back into Fitzjohn's Avenue. Small cobbled street, with
cafés either side.

Brian   Never go there. Don't know the place . . .

Edward   The sun, cutting a glare so bright I couldn't see his
face. But I instantly thought, just from the way he moved . . .
I thought, 'That looks like someone I know . . . God please
don't let it be him . . .' I just had this fear . . . Why be scared
of someone you associated with in school. Why? I thought
. . . it's just my imagination . . . Some misplaced fear. For
what? So went to find a table . . . And yep. It was him.

Brian   Bap-fucking-tiste . . .

Edward   And it's a Sunday. I look an absolute state . . .
Same clothes as the night before. Unwashed since the Friday.
So I'm there thinking. OK. Best thing I can do is keep
walking . . . I didn't want to speak to him. So I'm looking at
the houses for sale on this estate agent's window. Slowly
trying to turn back around the other way, and I hear . . .
'Hey Gilbert'. I turn. I can't see his face, the sun in my eyes,
but I see his head. Next to him, the hair of his very pretty
looking friend. Wife as I found out. Two children running
around. These cute golden coloured little things. 'Gilbert.'
Says it again. I smiled at him. In that very British . . .

Brian   Times like that I wish I was French. They don't give a flying shit . . . 'Pardon, and fuck off, Monsieur!' None of this reticent, hiding our feelings bollocks . . . I don't like you. And your life. It's upsetting me, and I'm gonna say it. You know what I mean? Should've done that.

Edward   But I'm walking up to him, thinking what on earth I'm going to say. Was I supposed to talk to him like . . . 'Hey, what's happening bro . . .' That type of . . . you know? (*Slight pause.*) Remember how he used to bully the hell out of us with his little 'Afro-Caribbean' gang . . . But his wife . . . Real trophy. Wow . . . Posh, everything. Definitely rich.

Brian   Rich tarts love a bit of the exotic . . . My parents, both from Telford. They really did me a favour and a half, you know what I mean?

Edward   Before I get a chance to say anything, even hello, I say the most stupidest thing. First thing I said . . . Pointing to the two little things, 'Wow these must be your . . .' as if it wasn't so obvious, the kids were mixed . . .

Brian   Would've done the same thing . . .

Edward   I was indirectly asking if that girl he was with was his wife. Because it was impossible. She's stunning . . .

Slight pause. They drink.

Edward   I was tired anyway. Couldn't sleep the night before. Insomnia. Mind was slow. Froze . . . Didn't know what to say beyond that . . . Tumbleweed moment . . . Lasted an hour. Or felt like . . . Just there standing . . . And he pulls out a chair . . .

Brian   Hate it when that happens.

Edward   Introduces his wife. Clare. And children. Esme and Alma. Twins. Perfect looking family . . . Family pet too . . . Little spaniel . . . named Puck. I mean, what the fuck?

Brian   Cunts . . .

Edward   And the bottle he was drinking, Verve Clicquot Rosé. On a Sunday. Twelve midday.

Brian   What man drinks that? You know what man drinks that? Someone with no culture . . . It's like these Chinese with their designer bags . . . Tacky . . . Money, yeah I get it . . . Like it means something.

Edward   . . . Almost finished, and so the second stupid thing I say . . . 'Hey another bottle, on me'. Don't ask me why I did that, but I did. A hundred and forty pounds . . . Half my weekly salary, gone.

Brian   It's only money . . .

Pause.

Edward   Told me how happy he was to see me. Genuine. You know, could see it in his eyes. Invited me to his house-warming later this week. Said I had to come along. Only lived five minutes walk away, in this huge town house. Four floors, balcony, just renovated, gym in the basement . . . Get this . . . one floor, the whole floor, a playroom for his two little . . . babies.

Brian   That's the problem with these finance people. You make a fortune, give it to them, they lose it all and still make money. Both in and out the door . . . Who wants that life . . .? It's theft!

Edward   Good looking wife. Beautiful kids . . . Gym in his basement . . .

Brian   Probably has herpes . . .

Long pause.

Brian   I'm bitching aren't I?

Edward   It's . . . No. Both of us. I . . .

Brian   . . . And I apologise. If I hadn't drunk so much, wouldn't've said something so low . . .

Edward   I know.

Brian   Wouldn't be so liberal with my thoughts but . . .

Edward   Alcohol is a wicked thing . . .

Brian   It is. But it's your fault. I'm having a good time . . .
Then you, bringing up Baptiste.

Pause.

What a cunt. Really . . . Basement with a gym? But I should
have more dignity than that.

Edward   Looked very good though . . . Healthy. Not worn
down by life at all.

Brian   He was one ugly sod . . .

Edward   First to lose his virginity . . .

Brian   Yeah exactly. How?

Long pause.

You get out much?

Edward   Me?

Brian   Yes, you.

Edward   Never . . .

Brian   No?

Edward   Today . . . first time . . . Hey, we haven't spoken in
how long . . . ?

Brian   When you least expect to hear from someone.

Edward   Yes. Your number. Found it. Had to call . . .

Brian   Of all people. Fucking Ed Gilbert . . . Eddy.

Edward   Doing well yourself too. Criminal law now . . . I
mean . . .

Brian   Well . . . Yeah.

Edward   Good job, good pay . . . Recession buster . . . Who doesn't need representation? Austerity . . . ? Whatever. People are still getting arrested for dumb shit.

Brian   Say that again . . . But I work for every penny. Represent Romanians mainly . . .

Edward   Really?

Brian   Come here, buy a car, no insurance . . . Think they're at home! . . . Don't understand why they've been brought to court. Soon as I finish representing them, I'm heading back to file for costs against them . . . Don't want to pay up. They think it's an entitlement. That it didn't cost someone's time. Cos the laws here . . . ? Stupid to them. Why pay . . . ? You know?

Edward   No respect . . .

Brian   'Got no money, I'm broke bla bla.' Fuck it . . . There's no kindness to be had without you doing something for someone, let's face it.

Edward   Got your own firm though. No easy thing . . .

Brian   I rent a small office in the backstreets of Wembley . . . Took the plunge. Set out on my own. (*Slight pause.*) But hey . . . One paralegal, a trainee. Nice Indian girl. Big tits . . . If she wasn't married . . . But that's it, very small team. Criminal work, from time to time, but mostly traffic stuff. We're breaking even . . . Not like the money we made before . . .

Edward   Study so you can be rich . . . ? Don't think so.

Brian   Bigger bitch than an STD.

Edward   Need money . . . ? Go back to sleep. Keep dreaming.

Brian   Drink to that . . .

Long pause.

Edward   One more?

Brian   Why not.

Edward   Same again?

Brian   Anything but that . . .

Edward   Didn't like the mix?

Brian   Drinking too much gin lately . . . Don't know why I asked for that in the first place . . . Done it all . . . Vodka, whiskey . . . mulled wine . . . port . . . rum. Don't drown your sorrows in gin. Nasty stuff. Got intimate with the toilet bowl at the Black Lion . . . My mouth smelt like ammonia for a week. Piss mouth. Bad memories . . .

Edward   Pile up the older we get, eh . . . ?

Brian   Sometimes wish I was a religious nut . . . Piss your life away, then have an afterlife full of scattered arse.

Brian *gets up, walks around, inspecting the flat.*

I like your place.

Edward   Thanks.

Brian   Not being an inverted snob here, but you've really come up the social ladder.

Pause.

I was smart . . . But why I spent my time chasing every woman . . . I just did finance, you know? Computing when I left school. I'd be living in St John's Wood.

Edward   Yeah.

Brian   Hampstead. Some million pound pad . . .

Edward   Yes.

Brian   Gym in my basement. Blonde wife like Bap-fucking-tiste. (*Pause.*) He is a cunt, isn't he. Feels good to say it. And you know it.

Pause.

Brian Yeah . . . Nice set up here . . . I'm jealous.

Edward Come on . . .

Brian Look at this flat . . . You know I did think about you once and wondered . . . What the hell became of Eddie Gilbert . . . ? Look at it. Thirty-four, and you've got a three bedroom flat . . . I couldn't raise a deposit for your toilet. Jealous. I'm sorry to admit, but I am. What I have? A studio. I get out of my bed, I'm standing by the sink. I'm brushing my teeth my dick is knocking against the microwave . . . Perfect training if you're planning to be an astronaut.

Edward We only moved here once Linda was pregnant. Her parents . . . The deposit . . . bye-bye to my writing career. PGCE. Mortgage. Monthly salary, two thirds of it gone before it hits your account. Not so glamorous.

Brian In-laws have to be good for something, eh? Anyway . . . You. . . . Young daughter . . . Never imagined it . . .

Edward Yeah. Nice . . . When I get to see her . . .

Brian You don't . . . ? Work hours?

Edward No . . . Nothing . . . I'm drunk.

Brian But you don't see her because?

Edward Yes. Work hours.

Brian Ah . . .

Edward Yeah . . . Teaching starts at eight. Out at seven. She's asleep. Back at nine, Linda's in bed, asleep with her. Good set-up. Get back, finish marking, couple glasses of wine. TV . . .

Brian Yes . . .

Edward Not what I thought 'family' would be . . . But . . .

Brian   Partial to a bit of that . . . TV. Obviously the late night stuff . . . Casino . . . Naked women. Tits bouncing around. Couple beers! Wrist sprain.

They both laugh. Pause.

Edward   And you?

Brian   What?

Edward   Relationship? Child, children you have? Don't know you have . . . Ha!

Brian   Nope . . . Relationships . . . ? In and out of them? I don't commit.

Edward   Out of fear?

Brian   Nah. Work is life. Women are fun. How I see it.

Edward   I remember you being the dog of the group; me, you, Patrick Durkan, Terry.

Brian   Terry!

Edward   Remember that time we went up to Liverpool, you disappeared the whole night with that German student with braids . . . Missed lectures the next morning. Almost got yourself suspended . . .

Brian   I don't fuck anymore . . . Those days are over.

Edward   You're single . . . Free.

Brian   Ejaculation . . . My biggest . . .

Edward   There are things you can take for that . . . I mean if you . . .

Brian   No . . . I can . . .

Edward   Sorry I . . .

Brian   Yes. No, it's . . . No it's not. Am I drunk?

Edward   Are you no. Yes!

Brian   The first time we meet in what? Seven years? And
I'm talking about ejacu-fucking-lation. Or lack of. For
spunk's sake.

Edward   Nothing shocks me. I work with teenagers.

Brian   I prefer to get my nut off alone. What I meant to say.
But that sounds very fucked up.

Edward   It does, yes.

Brian   Yeah.

Edward   And that's the reason? Why you haven't settled
down?

Brian   No. It's . . . I don't know what I'm saying.

Edward   Come on . . . Sorry. I'm probing. But you let an
interesting cat out of the bag . . .

Brian   It's private. And I'm too fucking drunk to keep my
mouth closed, and like the stupid cunt I am, I'm gonna tell
you. Jesus Christ.

Edward   Let me guess: you fall asleep, just at the moment
you're about to let off the shotgun . . . Piss the woman off
. . .? She leaves . . . you feel . . .

Brian   No, every time . . . I found myself . . . (*Slight pause.*) I
see ghosts . . . Death

Edward   OK. (*Pause.*) Really?

Brian   Really . . .

Edward   Ah . . . As a turn on . . . ? And morally it puts you
off the whole sexual experience . . . Necrophil . . .

Brian   . . . No, Jesus! What do you think I am? No . . . I'm
there with my eyes closed and you know I'm about to,
beautiful chick on top of me . . . you know, last time it
happened. Nice girl . . . Rebecca something . . . There's this
. . . This flashback thing. As if I'm dying. And I see all the
things in my life. Mind filled with thoughts. All there coming

back to me. Some girl I was with when I was seventeen, that I cheated on, and lied to, and stole money from . . . I'm being candid here . . . Some friend of my mum's I wish I'd been able to . . . all of them, all these people. And in the middle of them all . . . in the middle this . . . this . . . teenager . . . this dead. (*Slight pause.*) I just see his dead body . . . Just looking at me waiting for me to, you know . . . Like he's saying, go on do it . . . I dare you . . . Dare you to do it.

Pause.

Edward   Right . . . That is strange.

Brian   No I'm not . . . Not explaining myself . . .

Edward   Yes sure . . .

Brian   Not sexual . . . if you understand.

Edward   But you're ejaculating to the image of a dead teenage boy . . .

Brian   Not . . . no. He's there interrupting the thing. In my head there. Stopping me from . . . Some eighteen-year-old . . .

Edward   Someone you like, have seen on TV . . . ? I mean, I don't mind if you told me you were . . . homosex . . .

Brian   . . . No!

Edward   . . . Cos if you're . . .

Brian   I'm not! I'm . . . Some Somali kid.

Edward   What?

Brian   Who I represented once . . .

Edward   Some young Somali boy you represented holds you hostage from being able to let one out . . . now that is . . .

Brian   I'm serious . . .

Edward   You haven't been watching too many Japanese horror films . . . ?

Brian No . . .

Edward OK . . .

Pause.

Somali . . .

Brian How I met him . . . ? In real life . . . I was on duty. He was drunk. Name was Mo. I mean, couldn't walk. Couldn't stand up. Had veered out of his lane up by the A41, smashing into the car of a young couple. The man, twenty-one. Spine broken. Was in hospital, wasn't gonna walk again. I think.

Edward Jesus . . .

Brian Yeah. He's in the interview room. I'm trying to explain to him, that the reason why he was in the station was because he was arrested. Because he had caused serious injury by driving under the influence. And in this country . . . major offence. And for sure he was not getting bail, not getting out. Too drunk to take a breathalyzer test. (*Slight pause.*) Sat in the interview room, and I'm pretty much propping him up with my shoulder, advising the Custody Sergeant that my client doesn't want to say anything. Fuck having an interview . . . But he was obviously drunk, right? Couldn't've said shit anyway. All he did. All he did say . . . Very . . . Mumbled that he was Muslim. And it was some celebration and he was permitted to celebrate . . . Sort of . . . (*Slight pause.*) Haram . . . Something like that . . . And that's it. Went back to sleep.

Edward I mean, come on . . .

Brian Yeah, and as I was noting down everything from the disclosure I realized that he had an empty bottle of Evian in his car.

Edward But he's broken an innocent man's spine because he chose to drink and drive.

Brian Yes, that's what I . . .

Edward   . . . So of course, the book's gotta get thrown at him . . . And so it should . . . These fucking people . . .

Brian   But I'm his solicitor, I'm . . . I defend. I find reasons to defend. And yes he was guilty. Of course he was. Of course. But I knew that if he had drunk that bottle of water before he'd driven, he would have been drunk, but technically wouldn't have been over the legal limit. If I could prove . . .

Edward   But . . .

Brian   Yes. But I'm his solicitor . . . and I've got to use what I've got . . . And they're coming down on him like a ton of bricks. Strip searched, you name it. But I need to build my reputation. Reputation of my firm. If I can get this kid off, we're opening a new market here. All those Somali's that need legal advice, they'd all come to me. Make a decent living . . . I'd be the man that walks on water to these people.

Edward   Yes, but the law . . .

Brian   Which is exactly what it is . . . My version of events versus theirs . . .

Edward   And so . . . ?

Brian   I got him off . . . He was drunk. Yes. But I asked for a blood test . . . That bottle of water could've diluted the level of alcohol in his blood, I knew he would have been considered within the limit. It's all about the concentration of fluid in your body . . . And I advised him that he didn't have to tell me that he 'drank' at all. But it could have been equally plausible that he had maybe had one drink. Spiked, something . . . He was technically Muslim . . . He didn't drink. Who would argue? You take any religious argument into court, the judges are falling over each other not knowing what to do, it's easy . . . (*Slight pause.*) And while driving he had an attack of some kind, because alcohol is alien to his body because he's religious and . . . lost sight of where he was going, didn't see the car beside him and he veered into them.

Edward   And you got him off?

Brian   In the end, yes. Threw it out of court. Not guilty.

Edward   And yet, you know that he . . .

Brian   World we live in . . .

Edward   And the other man?

Brian   Paralyzed. As I later found out.

Pause.

Met his girlfriend. Both biologists at Imperial. Due to go to California, some research scholarship and he was . . . his life . . . He'd just passed his exams, had gone out for dinner. She'd persuaded him to go out. A surprise thing . . . And here I am, in the middle of this, having to balance, the 'law' and fairness, when there is nothing fair and yes it was the 'law', but it was me . . . It was my actions, and . . . I was thinking of myself. But what do you do? We're not brought up to think of others. We tell ourselves that we *care* but we're not . . . That's the thing about it . . . This place we live in right now . . . the 'western world,' whatever you wanna call it . . . we're fanatics too . . . We've got all this choice. Choose your career. Want a holiday, whatever . . . Gratification junkies. Everyone's rushing saying, 'I want this, that', perfect marriage, wedding, job . . . Cos we can have all this stuff we want so easy. When we get it, we don't even know what to do . . .

Edward   Bit pessimistic.

Brian   It's the fucking truth . . . That's why you got all this shit, fussing over climate change . . . ? All this other shit to fix . . . ? Can't fix ourselves, that's why . . .

Pause.

Brian   Anyway, I got a few more jobs from his people, whole bunch of Somali's calling me. Housing problems. Immigration things . . . Some community leaders beating their wives and having ABH charges against them. Things like that . . . But . . . I don't know, I lost the motivation.

Edward To . . . ?

Brian Couldn't go into the office . . .

Pause.

Edward Did your job

Brian I know, did a shit job.

Edward Got him off. That's the job. What you were supposed to do.

Brian He was guilty, I knew it. No sense of justice . . . (*Pause.*) Don't know. Thought I could talk to him.

Edward Did you?

Pause.

Brian To an extent. Contacted him a month later . . . Completely changed his life around. Was devout as you can get. When I first met him, wore track pants and a baseball cap. Now . . . ? The whole thing . . . that gown thing. First thing he said, kept talking about how fucked up his life was . . . Mum killed herself. Dad was in prison, for piracy in Kenya of all things . . . Don't know, after meeting him a few more times, giving him a bit of advice here and there . . . Don't know, saw me as an older brother. Father maybe . . . For this thing I did for him . . . Second chance at life.

Edward So he was . . . like Muslim, Muslim, now. Not the same

Brian Way this place is. You black or you're Jewish or Bengali. Whatever. Why associate with anyone that ain't you . . . ? Stop relating, you know? Keep to yourselves. Can't relate . . . And I'm an adaptable guy. More adaptable than I think. But I just . . . After a while didn't get it. I never had a clear reason why a few months ago he was like me, have small talk about what drinks we'd get smashed on . . . Bars that had the loosest girls . . . And then all of a sudden it's a sin to suddenly sip a beer . . . What the fuck? And we're in a pub and I'm trying to get him to . . . a little half pint. But it's as if he's of some special higher existence mission now. And even the way he looked at me. Sees me pick up a pint and he's watching that 'poison' I'm ingesting. Could see it in his eyes. That judgement.

Edward   For the better though . . . at least he'd changed.

Brian   No . . . I don't know. Could understand where he was coming from, before . . . Some youngster who basically fucked up. But . . . This? (*Pause.*) One night I was drunk, heavy day at work, the usual, clearing my head. He calls me, said meet him in East London.

Edward   You went?

Brian   So I went. Trying not to stagger. And I walk up Whitechapel, met him, his friends, young Somalis, all Muslim. And these boys have seen war . . . It's in their . . . You can't talk to them the same way, you or I . . . I mean. I talk about how much I fucking hate this country, but, really? The way they were . . . ? (*Pause.*) It was calm, not reactive, and there's all this proof why they should hate a lot of shit here . . . Who wouldn't? Who wouldn't? The Queen, with her fleet of Range Rovers. Shit like that. Our government making decisions for us. People they don't have a clue about . . . They wanted it to come all crashing down. Saying how they wanted to light up the place. Like some fuck-off explosion taking us right back to zero. (*Pause.*) We end up going to this mosque and I'm . . . I'm getting involved. I'm too damn drunk to know what the hell is going on, and they all knew that, but they didn't mind. They show me how to wash. And I'm in this gigantic room, at evening prayers, with all these people. Kneeling. Standing up. Kneeling. And I felt my body for the first time. So intoxicated with all this shit, I put in it. Things I'd done . . .

Edward   You're going to tell me you're religious now?

Brian   Me? No . . . I was cleansed for a bit . . . I was, for about five minutes till I reached Shoreditch. (*Slight pause.*) I don't know. Maybe it was a few weeks after, I was having a coffee. And an acquaintance. Some conspiracy theory junkie, he tells me that the police, they pay for intelligence, for information on radicals . . . So I called them . . .

Edward   Jesus.

Brian   I don't know. Two young students their lives ruined, and this boy, given a chance to start again. And me being the one who somehow upset the natural order of things. I felt I had to balance it out. If the police took one look at these boys and the things they were talking about. The anger they all had . . . They'd be taken off the street . . . And that was a balance of justice . . . I had to . . . (*Slight pause.*) So I had them call me on this number, you know, they're asking . . . 'Where are you now?' They wanted to meet me right there and then. Have some police car pull up, question me in detail. (*Slight pause.*) And the first thing I was thinking was, fuck me! What shit was on my computer . . . What was . . . porn I'd looked at, 'school girls' stuff like that. Stuff that I had on my mind . . . And so I had to rush home, do something. Told me they were gonna do background checks on me. Make sure I wasn't concealing information from them. I mean really.

Edward   You live a very eventful life.

Brian   Oh I know! And I knew they were coming to my place. I couldn't do it in time, erase all the little entries in my computer. Had a brand new Mac too. Panicked. Ended up smashing it to pieces . . . Smashed it to bits. My attempt at trying to convey myself as an upstanding citizen. But who the hell is?

Edward   I've been there . . .

Brian   Where?

Edward   Would I get arrested for shit I do in private . . .

Pause.

Brian   And the worst thing of it all . . . They didn't call me back.

Edward   They didn't?

Brian   Not a call . . . No. Nothing. Didn't bother even coming around. Thought I was just wasting their time.

Edward   But you smashed your computer . . .

Brian   Yes, with all my dates, appointments, you name it . . . And all the no-shows in court for about a month because my diary was in there. Started losing money. Rent for the office was due and I just couldn't cover it. Lost all these clients . . . I'm still a solicitor . . . But all I seem to have now is the qualification. Haven't practiced in . . . (*Slight pause.*) That balance of justice, it happened . . . it was me it happened to . . .

Pause.

Edward   You know something . . . Of all the weeks in the year, this is the worst week. They say . . .

Brian   Really?

Edward   Yeah . . . The most suicides in the year . . . This month. They say out of this week, that this is the most depressing day of that week . . . Imagine . . .

Brian   Think they're right, look at me.

Edward   And I always thought Mondays were the worst though . . . Always . . . But it's not . . . Tuesday.

Brian   Every day sucks dick right now.

Edward   Think about it? You spend the weekend smashed, self loathing whatever, feel the blues Sunday. Tell yourself Monday will be rough but better. Get through that day. Tuesday you'll be back on form. But sometimes, by the time Tuesday comes . . . and . . . If you know, by then you're still just the same. Still drinking, still fucked . . . Self loathing . . . You know the rest of the week, it's a write off.

Long pause.

Brian Fucking Tuesdays . . .

Silence.

Edward So the reason why you saw that boy as a ghost? You never told me . . . What happened to him?

Brian Stopped speaking to him. After I made that call . . . Had many missed calls. Didn't answer. Then I get this call from some. Someone trying to identify his body. . . . I'd been the last number on his speed dial . . . They called me. The police . . . Asked me if I knew him . . . Turns out, I was the last person he called . . . Before he . . . (*Pause.*) I remember too . . . Watching TV, my phone, seeing his number . . . Twenty missed calls . . . didn't pick them up. Thought fuck him . . . Fuck you . . . you cunt . . . (*Slight pause.*) Back of my mind, knew he needed me.

Edward Did they ever tell you how he died?

Brian He lived on the eleventh floor. South Kilburn Estate . . . Jumped off.

Pause.

Edward Well.

Brian Yeah . . .

Edward Well . . .

Pause. **Edward** *picks up his phone.*

Edward (*calling someone*) Sorry, just need to.

Brian She due home soon?

Edward No.

Brian I give up, stupid, to get so drunk . . . things happen, and . . . Man, I just dumped on you.

Edward Sorry I should . . . (*On his phone, getting up. Sending a message.*)

Brian   Yes of course.

Pause. Sits back down. Putting phone down.

Should I?

Edward   Ah no.

Brian   Work tomorrow? Daughter to nursery. If she . . .

Edward   No daughter. She's at her grandparents.

Brian   Right.

Edward   Linda's gone out. Still out. It's fine.

Brian   Didn't seem like . . . Seemed like . . .

Edward   Like?

Brian   Maybe she's around the corner, you know? 'He still here.' That sort of thing.

Pause.

Edward   Ah no. She's not coming back. Not yet.

Brian   Because I'm here.

Edward   No . . . They spend all their lives being mothers. Need to be themselves. Need to live a bit . . .

Long silence.

Brian   I should go . . .

Pause.

Edward   One more?

Brian   Another drink I'd forget where I live. Not that I don't want to forget where I live . . . That's exactly what I want to do. But you wouldn't want me having to sleep here, trust me.

Edward   Ah . . .

Pause

Edward   Well.

Brian   Yes?

Slow fade.

Scene Two

Same place. Hours later. Lights off. **Edward** *is asleep on the sofa. A sudden racket can be heard from upstairs.* **Edward** *suddenly awake gets up. He turns the light on.* **Brian** *is stood in front of him. Coat on.*

Brian   Shouldn't be here.

Edward   It's my fault. I know.

Brian   Shouldn't . . . Where am I?

Edward   Kilburn . . . ish

Brian   Kilburn? Shit . . . What am I doing here?

Edward   Where I live?

Brian   Shit.

Edward   Want a cab . . . Can stay.

Brian   No, not a cab . . . walk . . . I'll walk will . . . not so far.

Edward   Really? . . . Go back to sleep. Shower in the morn. Got some spare shirts, should be the same fit. You try to walk to Wembley at this time, the state you're in?

Brian   What time is it?

Edward   Dunno . . . Late. So late it's early.

Brian   Fuck . . . (*Slight pause.*) Where is she?

Edward   Who?

Brian   Your wife?

Edward   Oh.

Brian   She's . . . I mean probably on her way home, about to open that door, some stranger here . . . Talking absolute shite.

Edward   Don't be stupid.

Brian   If she saw me . . . I mean if she did . . . 'Hey, you get out! Ed, don't bring homeless cunts into the house that you haven't seen for ten years!'

Edward   It's not been ten years, idiot.

Brian   Drunk!

Edward   You don't say. Fuck we overdid it.

Brian   Great idea to knock a few shots back.

Edward   You go rummaging in the cupboard, you always find a bottle of tequila someone bought you on their trip to Malaga.

Brian   Great idea. You know. Wasn't my idea.

Pause.

And don't get me wrong. I did try to sleep . . . don't get me wrong. Up there in your toilet, which is a toilet I can sleep in, trust me. I've had my head in so many toilets, I know a clean one when I see one . . . I'm ready to go to sleep, right there . . . But every time I close my eyes, tried to close my eyes, my head, spinning, keep waking up . . . Feel like I'm gonna throw up. Vicious cycle.

Edward   Don't wanna throw up there . . . Linda will kill you. Ha!

Brian   No way, wouldn't do that.

Edward   Dirty the carpet. Enough to start divorce proceedings, man. You want a bucket, I'm sure I can . . . I've got a . . .

Brian *tilts his head back. A silence.*

Edward   What are you doing?

Brian   Swallowing it back down . . . It's OK. I'm OK. . . . Wait . . . Dizzy spell . . .

Edward   Anyone you can call?

Brian   Police? Who?

Edward   No, to come and collect you . . . A friend?

Brian   I guess I could check my . . . (*Struggles to pull out his phone. Does so eventually.*) Should've said goodnight hours ago . . .

Edward   Sleep here. Don't let me say it again.

Brian   Yeah?

Edward   Yes. Trust me . . . One hell of a catch up. We'll meet up go to this house-warming in a few weeks' time. Laugh about how sick drunk we are right now . . .

Brian   OK . . .

Edward   Good . . .

Brian   Good . . .

Pause.

You know what?

Edward   What?

Brian   I'm fucking happy . . .

Edward   So am I!

Brian   Because I'm happy I'll stay . . .

Edward   Good!

Brian   A little bit. Only because you're forcing me to do this. In any other circumstance, I would be out of here, just letting you know that . . . (*Slight pause. He sits down again.*) Anyway, going home at this time of night. The place I stay in, you want to be indoors.

Edward   Why?

Brian   Studio flat I rent, right? Small flat in a bunch of them, narrow house that was converted into rooms. All rundown, but just about liveable. Rooms all partitioned, no walls, plasterboard on MDF, that type of shit . . . I've got some interesting neighbours.

Edward   You being one of them right?

Brian   Yep, got two prozzies . . .

Edward   Really?

Brian   Uh huh, same floor. Monika and Monique.

Edward   Nice.

Brian   Play all this Euro pop stuff. Don't know if they're fucking or dancing . . . Every few moments a scream.

Edward   Entertaining.

Brian   But you don't wanna go into the flat late . . . You have punters coming up to you. Asking where to go, like you're one of them. A punter . . . Happened to me once. I'm on my way upstairs, and this man is following me. Walked right into my flat behind me, looks around, only sees me in the flat then asks, 'Where the hell are the girls'? I'm not a faggot'. Calls me gay and storms out. (*Pause.*) Shitty rundown flats are always lucrative. If you're into that sort of thing. But not me . . . (*Slight pause.*) Money, not so lucky . . . not like you . . . Trust fund, Eddy!

Edward   I'm not.

Brian   Only parents I've got to help house me are Brent Council. You're in a council block there like a swarm of locusts . . . First thing, soon as you enter inside, a sign, saying no smoking, not that anyone follows that at all. Place stinks of cigarettes. Or some strange food smells, Polish, African . . . Kurdistani some shit . . .

Edward   Bit shit . . .

Brian   Yes it is. Not that you know what shit is . . . With this place . . .

Edward   What about it?

Brian   Price of it . . . You don't live in the same London I do, pal.

Edward   Whatever . . . Of course I do.

Brian   You don't. With your middle class enclave flat . . . for Ethiopian filter coffee drinking. Picturehouse cinema going . . . I know . . . This area . . . ? And the worst thing . . . They fucked us . . . fucking champagne liberals. And I'm supposed to be Labour through and through . . .

Edward   Who knows what Labour is now . . . From the moment Tony . . .

Brian   No, fuck him, not talking about him! Don't give me that shit! Way before that . . . decades . . . This state-sponsored fucking multicultural fuck . . . As long as you live in your nice flat, eating your avocado toast like a wanker . . . what do you know?

Edward   Come on, that's a bit low.

Brian   You don't know what I'm talking about. Know what this whole things about?

Edward   Then tell me if you think . . .

Brian   They tell everybody, yeah identify with your neighbours, that's what we do . . . What we should be fucking proud of, as citizens of this great British . . . fuck it . . . people like you, identify only with people just like you . . . Close yourselves off. It's the rest of us . . .

Edward   School I work in . . . I see a lot of diverse . . .

Brian   No, don't fuck me off with that . . . ! Don't know what the fuck I'm talking about. Tired middle class and plastic, fucking disgusting . . .

Edward   Why would you say that?

Brian   Plastic life, look at you . . . Three in the morning . . .
Look at you . . . like you got a stick up your arse . . . I'm
smashed . . . You're humouring me . . .

Edward   Wait a minute . . .

Brian   I'm here talking all this shit . . . I wanna be out in
the desert somewhere screaming my fucking head off . . .
And you plastic bastard . . . Calm as fuck . . . Three in the
morning and your wife not even back, oh please . . . She still
out having fun with her pals? You believe that?

Edward   Out a lot, what she does.

Brian   Out with friends . . . ? All this time? Bollocks. Don't
lie to yourself . . .

Edward   Yes . . . Actually.

Brian   Well, you've gotta believe something . . . Don't
you . . .

Edward   Why are you being a cunt?

Brian   What? Telling you the truth . . . ? All this come over
look at my perfect life, perfect friends, perfect living, all
surface. You know what I hate about you? Everything has to
be so fucking perfect, even if everything is falling around
you, you'll pretend it isn't. Kill yourselves before you open
your eyes . . .

Edward   I'm sorry you hate your pathetic life, I really am.

Brian   Fuck, your sorry . . . Fuck you.

Edward   Go on . . . jog on, get going . . .

Brian   Yeah, you prick . . .

Edward   Waste of time . . .

Brian   I was Linda? I'd be doing the same fucking thing.
Who'd wanna keep having to open their legs to a fucking
plastic prick . . .

Edward *gets up instantly. Standing over* **Brian**.

Edward   Out!

Long silence. **Edward** *backs away, as* **Brian** *fumbles for his coat. He stops.*

Brian   Fuck . . . (*Long pause.*) Sorry.

Pause.

So sorry . . . Don't know where that all came from . . .

Pause.

Haha . . . I'm jealous. I'm just . . . The drink . . . Why do I have to go and . . .

Brian *tries to put his coat on but falls to the ground.* **Edward** *quickly attempting to get him up. Pause.*

Edward   Come on . . .

Brian   Yeah . . . outstayed my welcome . . .

Brian *gets up. Pushing* **Edward** *away.*

Brian   I'm fine . . . I'm . . . Fuck, I can get up . . .

Long pause. **Brian** *walks to the door. Stops.*

We're going still? Bap-fucking-tiste?

Pause.

You're not gonna call me again, are you?

Edward (*after a pause*)   I will.

Brian   Don't be a fucking cunt and change your mind on me . . .

Edward   Brian. I should get to bed . . .

Pause.

Brian   I'm fucking alone.

Edward   We'll rewind the clock . . . it'll be fun.

Brian   I think I'm an alcoholic, how would I meet someone? How? And be fucking sociable. Functional for a day max . . . I shouldn't be going to these places.

Edward   Matter of choice . . . Just don't drink till we get there . . . Both of us.

Brian   Both of us?

Edward   Yeah.

Brian   You'll come by . . . my office . . . Or I come here.

Edward   I'll come by the office . . . text me the address . . .

Pause. **Brian** *tries to retrieve his phone from his pocket.*

Edward   No later, when you get home . . . (*Slight pause.*) Right, cab numbers . . . They leave their cards downstairs by the front door. I'll come down, ring . . .

Brian   No . . . No. I . . . I didn't bring my wallet with me . . .

Edward   That's fine, I'll spot you the fare.

Brian   I know where to . . . I can make my way . . . I . . .

Brian *stands by the door. He stops wants to say something. Doesn't. He exits.* **Edward** *closes the door behind him. He goes back to the table, picks up his phone. Calls. Nothing. Calls again. Puts his phone down. He downs the last of his drink. He goes out of the room, returns with a pillow and duvet.*

Edward (*to himself, almost under his breath*)   Fucking cunt! Self centered . . . ?

He makes his bed on the sofa. He checks his phone. Sighs. He pours himself another drink, puts the lid on the bottle. He downs it. He turns the light off. He pours himself another drink. Drinks only half of the contents. He puts the glass down. He pulls the duvet over his head.

Scene Three

Days later. Early morning. **Edward**, *in bed asleep, the duvet covering him. The door bell buzzes. It does so again.* **Edward** *suddenly jolts up. He wears only a t-shirt and boxers. He looks lost, doesn't know where he is. The door buzzes again. He gets up, checks to see who it is discreetly. Panics. Looks around him, the place is a state. Starts clearing up. The door buzzes again.* **Edward** *throws all the empty food packets, beer cans, bottles everything onto the table. Throws his duvet on top. Quickly he runs to the door. Opens it.* **Nic**, *her coat on, bag in hand enters. She stands by the door.*

A silence.

Nic   Should consider the gender of your guests . . . ? If I didn't know you . . . ? I'd feel very uncomfortable.

Edward (*suddenly noticing his lack of clothing*)   I didn't expect you to . . .

Nic   You've been calling non-stop.

Edward   Yes.

Nic   Didn't expect me to turn up? After the calls?

Edward   Sort of . . .

Nic   Or the messages . . . ? Early hour messages?

Edward   About those . . .

Nic   Drunk ones . . .

Edward   My inhibitions . . .

Nic   Obscene . . .

Edward   I'm sorry . . .

Nic   Married men and their 'sexting' habits . . . I say married, but . . .

Edward   I'm married.

Nic   Not what I've heard. But OK.

Long pause.

Edward   The calls . . . ?

Nic   Yes . . . ?

Edward   Needed to speak.

Nic   About . . . ?

Edward   At the time needed to . . . What about? Don't remember. But . . . You don't pick up.

Nic   Don't want to speak to you.

Edward   Can't I just pick up the phone these days . . . ?

Nic   If you do. I'm here to tell you . . .

Edward   OK. Won't call . . .

Nic   I will block your number.

Edward   What you came to tell me?

Nic   What I came to tell you . . .

Pause.

Edward   I was drunk, I apologise.

Long pause.

Nic   What's happened to you? You OK?

Edward   Yeah . . . Just getting my head around . . .

Nic   Around . . . ?

Edward   Some people, invite them over, they spend the night getting drunk at your expense. Then project all their bullshit onto you . . .

Nic   Some people?

Edward   Had a friend. Over the other day . . .

Nic   Ah . . .

Edward   Friend, hadn't seen in a long time . . . Tells me . . . (*Slight pause.*) Do you mind if I tell you . . .

Nic   Continue . . .

Edward   This friend, we were having a good time . . . (*Slight pause.*) Tells me . . . I'm self-centred . . .? The fuck . . .? That true about me?

Nic   I see, need a second opinion . . .? Why you called?

Edward   Not just that . . .

Nic   I'll just call Nic . . . Cos someone's said something horrible to me.

Edward   No.

Nic   And when I get ignored I'll tell her how much I want to fuck.

Long pause. **Nic** *laughs to herself.*

Edward   What's funny?

Nic   Nothing.

Edward   You're laughing at me.

Nic   I'm not laughing . . . Smirking maybe . . . something . . . Impression I had of you in my mind.

Edward   Haven't cut my hair in a while . . . that's funny? Need a shave. Yes, I get it.

Nic   Reminds me of . . . Know what it reminds me of?

Edward   Don't know. Should I know?

Nic   I was on the bus, saw this young girl, yesterday. This child, maybe three, four. Wanted to sit on one seat further up the bus from where the prams are in the middle. Her mother wouldn't let her. She's there pulling and pulling, her mum holding her arm. Her, making such a fuss trying to get away, screaming . . . screams so loud, making sure everyone could witness this injustice being done to her . . . And the bus, it stops abruptly, the momentum, she goes flying. Smack! Falls flat on her little button nose. Gets up . . . Doesn't cry . . . But when she looks around at everybody, then back to her mother. Her mother with this, 'I told you so' look on her face . . . This publically embarrassing moment . . . She just lets out the loudest cry, inconsolable . . .

Edward   What I remind you of?

Nic   What I think about, yes. Right here looking at you.

Pause.

Edward   What time is it?

Nic   Early.

Edward   Sun ain't fully up. Very early.

Nic   Someone's been enjoying the lie-ins. The 8 ams were like lunchtimes for us once . . .

Edward   They were . . . Up at five. Marking . . . with hangovers . . . Black coffee . . . Yeah.

Pause.

Nic (*noticing the table*)   Do you always put your duvet on top of your coffee table like that? On top of what looks like a couple beer cans, packets of Pringles . . .

Edward *quickly tries to neaten the duvet; he doesn't take it off the table.*

Edward   On your way to work?

Nic   We can't all get up when we want.

Edward   How's the department?

Nic   OK . . . We're doing fine.

Edward   A lot of kids I've got a good relationship with . . .

Nic   Harry . . .

Edward   You all don't like to think that but . . .

Nic   Harry.

Edward   Taken over my class . . . ?

Nic   Helps a lot of them. Pretty good at picking up where you left off . . . Doing a better job than I thought . . . Ofsted.

Edward   What do they know . . .

Nic   He got a fifty-seven per cent pass rate last term . . . Your best was thirty-nine.

Edward   It's still my . . .

Nic   He might take over the department . . . They've offered it to him.

Pause.

Edward   He's the 'writer', isn't he?

Nic   Let me read the first chapter of his new novel . . .

Edward   Teen fiction . . . (*Mild sarcasm.*) Digs from a deep well, doesn't he?

Nic   Everything has to be wrought in blood, does it?

Edward   Anyone can do that . . . That's all . . .

Nic   And teach at the same time? (*Pause.*) Got an advance, HarperCollins . . . Thriller . . .

Edward   Fuck off . . . No way.

Nic   Yeah.

Edward   Really?

Nic   Yeah.

Edward   Disliked him before. But now? Hate him!

Nic   Know what his novel's about?

Edward   Go . . . Gotta hear this . . .

Nic   It's set in this dystopian . . . something . . .

Edward   Wow . . .

Nic   Female protagonist, no race . . .

Edward   Very current . . . Speaks to us 'underrepresented types' . . .

Nic   Religio-political undertones, I don't get it but . . .

Edward   It sounds awful . . .

Nic   . . . But it's very funny.

Pause.

Edward   Yeah. (*Pause.*) I'd like to read it . . . (*Pause.*) Does he still put his dumb classic FM on in the staff room. Write in the breaks . . .?

Nic   All the fucking time . . .

Edward   Forgot to close his laptop once, remember? The amount of mileage we had on that opening paragraph he wrote . . . 'The yellow tulips . . .

Nic   . . . Blossoming' . . .

Edward   . . . Blossoming . . . Such a shitty script . . .

Nic   He's got a lot better now.

Pause.

Edward   Want a cup of tea?

Nic   I'm fine . . .

Edward   I'll take your coat . . . Come sit down . . .

Nic   No thanks, rather keep it on. Lots to do at the office before the kids come in.

Pause.

Edward   OK, so . . . As I was saying . . . Met a friend . . . I invited him to this house-warming . . . school reunion type thing . . . friend whose party it is, really successful now . . .

It's in a few weeks. You came into my mind. I want you to come. Instead. (*Slight pause.*) Won't get him to come . . . make some excuse . . . (*Slight pause.*) No fucking way, I won't call him . . . what a cunt . . .

Nic   I can't, I'm sorry.

Edward   I'm being too harsh . . .? I'm being harsh. (*Slight pause.*) Think about it, it'd be . . . We'll have a good time . . . But . . .

Pause.

Read in the local paper, they're changing the college into an academy . . .?

Nic   Doesn't affect us.

Edward   It could, in the future . . . Parents having their say in areas they shouldn't.

Nic   Feel bad saying this . . .

Edward   Feel bad? What . . .?

Nic   They've been talking about it . . .

Edward   They?

Nic   You've not got a job there. Anymore . . . I'm surprised you don't know already . . .

Edward   . . .. Taking time off. To write my novel . . .

Nic   Novel . . .?

Edward   What I'm doing . . . They called a few times, didn't wanna deal with it . . . I will . . . They can't just . . .

Nic   It's been eleven months . . .

Edward   Like I said . . . Taking time to write . . .

Nic   God, you're actually talking as if what you're doing is normal . . . It's . . .

Edward   So Harry got an advance . . . Yeah, good . . . Send my congratulations . . .

Nic   . . . Ed . . .

Edward   Not that he needs it . . . You go to Cambridge, say you wanna write about the different colour toilet seats you piss into for example . . . some publisher's gonna . . .

Nic   He went to East Anglia.

Edward   Same thing . . . You're defending him . . . Used to hate him . . . Way you describe what he's doing, sounds like he's just ticking boxes . . . that's not writing, that's marketing . . . You read Rilke . . .

Nic   . . . Didn't come here to be ranted at.

Edward   What's wrong with you?

Nic   Why should something be wrong with me?

Edward   You two . . . Kinda close now?

Nic   It's none of your business.

Edward   Yep, it's none of my . . . OK . . .

Long pause. **Nic** *looks around.*

Nic   So this is your place? What it looks like?

Edward   Want me to take you around, show you every detail . . . Colour of the skirting boards . . .

Nic   I'm glad I never came here . . .

Edward   Could've any time you wanted . . . Your choice not to . . .

Slight pause.

Nic   Was getting ready to come here . . . this morning . . . putting my clothes on . . . and this . . . Suddenly I was back, maybe a year . . . Like taking an old coat out the wardrobe . . . (*Slight pause.*) This whole thing . . .

Edward   What thing?

Nic   What I used to do . . . get dressed early . . . come, wait for you . . .

Edward   What colleagues do . . .

Nic   Wait at the bottom of the road . . . Hated that I never saw what this place looked like . . .

Edward   Like I said, your choice . . .

Nic   I'd meet you on the corner . . . We'd walk to work. I'd always pop into the shop beforehand, so it didn't look as if we were going in together . . .

Edward   Way things happen . . .

Nic   Way you wanted it . . .

Edward   If that's how you want to remember . . .

Nic   Don't be a prick with me. Don't . . .

Pause.

Nic   You have no right . . .

Long pause.

Edward   You don't see someone for a while, but what does it diminish? . . . (*Slight pause.*) Know what I remember? I remember how, we'd be in the staff room . . . soon as you'd come in, put your feet up on the coffee table in there . . . Everyone hated it . . . used to keep me in hysterics, such a tomboy thing to do . . . but these things about you . . .

Nic   Reminiscing . . .

Edward   Pardon me?

Nic   What this is about? Eleven months, nothing . . . Suddenly . . .

Edward   I wasn't. . .

Nic   What next? You gonna talk about some time you sat with me on Primrose Hill? Played with my hair, or some other sentimental . . . piece of shit story . . .

Edward   No, I never . . .

Nic   I'll just bulldoze my way to get what I want from her. Feed her my best short stories of the great old times . . . Invite her to a party . . .

Edward   I'm trying to be nice . . .

Nic   Nice?

Edward   OK, I get it, yeah, we're strangers now . . .

Nic   It's been a year . . . yes!

Edward   The way I cut you off . . . It was wrong.

Nic   Why are you telling me this?

Edward   It's what you deserve to hear.

Nic   It's weird. It's so fucking male. It's offensive.

Edward   What the fuck is your problem?

Nic   You must think I need you . . .

Edward   Why come here then?

Nic   I know. Forget this, I don't give a shit.

Nic *turns towards the door.*

Edward   I miss the old times . . .

Nic   Yeah, sorry to hear that . . .

Edward   Nic, please.

Nic   You're a prick.

Edward   Yes, OK, I can be that . . .

Nic   You are, and it's not charming, there is no charm. If you were better looking, maybe, just maybe I'd put up with it, would find it palatable . . . but you?

Edward   Why do us men have to fit into . . .

Nic   I regret giving myself to you . . .

Edward   Don't talk like that . . . That's not true. I hurt you and I'm sorry. You have a right to be nasty to me . . . but we had something, it was close . . .

Nic   You make my work life a misery. How long have I been there now? Third year now? First job . . . So young . . . you're this . . . you're confident, flirtatious. . . What did you say . . . 'Don't you dare show how you feel about me, Nic', what you used to say . . . Snap at me that I show you the slightest bit of public affection, scold me for it . . .

Edward   I said that?

Nic   Don't tell anyone that we have what we have, but when I want you, when I really want you, I'll text you, give you a look, get you to meet me in the computer room cos I'll have the keys.

Edward   My actions, if I did that, don't tell the full picture . . . I'm putting my life back together . . . you're part of that.

Pause.

She called . . .

Nic   Who?

Edward   Linda . . . (*Pause.*) I want my family back . . .

Nic   What are you? You don't know what the fuck that is . . .

Edward   I know what . . .

Nic   What I know . . .? I never met her but she was smart . . . smart to smell your bullshit and walk away . . .

Edward   Everyone needs a break.

Nic   Whatever this place is, it's not a home. She's not coming back.

Edward   I'm sorry you want to believe that . . . (*Pause.*) I just . . . Let's keep the good friendship we had . . . Move forward, put the mistakes to one side . . . (*Slight pause.*) Want you to meet her . . .

Nic (*slight pause; laughs*)   Pick up where we left off . . . ?

Edward   I miss our friendship. My job, my life. This is my home; this is my place.

Nic   What about your daughter?

Edward   What about her?

Nic   Say nothing about her? Where is she in this . . . ? When's the last time you saw her?

Edward   This isn't about that . . . She's with her grandparents. . . by the coast . . . Not the easiest to get down there.

Nic *laughs to herself.*

Edward   What? You find it funny? What's fucking funny?

Slight pause.

Nic   You wanted to write, you talked about it so much . . . (*Pause.*) You always talk about doing something . . . I helped pay for your office, your printer, paper, books. I facilitated your lies . . . didn't I?

Edward   They weren't lies . . .

Nic   All the time, late I'd call you, ask you how it was going . . . were you gonna meet your deadline, you'd always keep pushing them back . . . coming to mine, sleep, sometimes you'd be home . . . complain about not having the right atmosphere to create . . . Deep down, it's all a lie. What I realized . . . Why I had to come here . . . It's a lie . . . I lied too . . .

Edward   How?

Nic   About caring . . . I never . . .

Edward   What do you mean?

Nic   Moved to London, new job, new people, I was alone
. . . I was bored, with you, without you . . . I just didn't want
to be alone . . . But I never cared.

Edward   If it makes you feel better to say that . . .

Nic   You think you have this hold over me . . .

Edward   You're here. I called, you came . . . You tell me?

Nic (*slight pause*)   I genuinely wanted to help you . . .

Edward   . . . I don't need that . . .

Pause.

Nic   You had this short story. You gave it to me to read . . . I
never read it, cos I never wanted to know . . . Who you were
. . . Like, if I read your stuff . . . Saw who you were . . . I'd
like you more . . . Your short story. I read it . . . And I get
what you're trying to do, this whole Salinger style thing. But
I just feel pity, it's awful. You're awful. I felt bad to think
that, and that made me care. (*Slight pause.*) Maybe . . . I . . .
(*Pause.*) You think you have this hold over me . . . How
hurting me somehow makes you something . . . ? I don't
want you to think that about me . . . I don't think about
you . . .

Edward   When you're ready to get back to the way things
were . . .

Nic   Don't ever call me again.

Edward   Nic . . .

Nic   No . . .

Edward   Please . . . just hear me out.

Nic   I've gotta go to work.

Nic *reaches for the door.*

Edward   You don't just fucking leave people! You don't!

Nic   You should clean up.

Edward   I'm a fucking person.

Nic *opens the door.*

She exits. **Edward** *remains where he is, unable to move.*

Slow fade.

Scene Four

Day. Weeks later. **Edward** *dressed up sits at the table.* **Linda** *stands by the sofa, she's looking for something.*

Linda   Royal Dalton.

Edward   Royal what?

Linda   Teapot.

Edward   Oh.

Linda   I asked you especially.

Edward   That ugly thing . . . You hated it.

Linda   Yeah, well . . .

Edward   Always had it in the back of the cupboard.

Linda   My mum wants it back.

Edward   Right.

Linda   Crystal glasses too . . .

Edward   Behind the sofa.

Linda   Where? On top or underneath these empty bottles?

Edward   Under . . . (*Slight pause.*) Was doing a spot of spring cleaning . . . Waiting to recycle.

Linda *keeps looking amongst the things on the sofa.*

Edward   Can you see it? I'll get up.

Linda   No it's OK.

Edward   It's there . . . Where I put it . . . (*Getting up.*) Fuck's sake . . .

Linda   It's OK, I'll find it.

Edward   Gonna be late, you'll take forever . . .

Linda   Going out for lunch?

Edward   No, for tonight . . .

Linda   Tonight . . . ? It's the afternoon.

Edward   Preparing early . . .

Linda   OK . . . Punctual. Very good.

Edward   Yes. Always.

Long pause.

Bumped into an old friend.

Linda   Good for you.

Edward   Friend from school.

Linda   Good. (*Looking through boxes.*) Hope my things aren't thrown out, Ed.

Edward   No, of course not. (*Pause.*) Think he's the right person to go with? Take to this house-warming with me?

Linda   Don't know. Was he your bezzy mate back then?

Edward   Sort of.

Linda   Take him why not.

Edward   Maybe . . . That's if I go.

Linda   Should get out more, meet new people.

Pause. **Edward** *helps* **Linda** *look through boxes.*

Linda   Teapot . . . Can't find it.

Edward   It's somewhere . . . (*Pause.*) These things . . . for your mum's place?

Linda   No, new place. Cupboard empty, think it will do OK. Something to fill it.

Pause.

Edward   Should get out more . . .

Linda   Sorry?

Edward   That you being malicious?

Linda   For what reason . . . (*Picking up a box.*) Ah yes, the crystal. So you did pack them.

Edward   Fucking heartless thing to say.

Linda   Pardon me?

Edward   Meet new people . . .

Linda   A suggestion only . . .

Edward   I've got friends.

Linda   Good, I'm happy.

Edward   It's not all a conveyor belt of people. Pick up and dump as and when.

Linda   I wasn't trying to offend you.

Edward   Offended . . . ? I'm not offended . . . Don't get offended.

Pause.

Linda   Tea? I'll make myself some. You want?

Edward   I'm OK . . . No.

Linda   I'll make you some. Rooibos still in?

Edward   Have to check.

Linda   I'll go look . . . Shouldn't be so dismissive, tea's good for you. Especially the low caffeine stuff.

Linda *exits the room.*

Linda (*from kitchen*)   Nothing's used in here. Don't you cook?

Edward   Sometimes.

Long pause.

Linda (*from kitchen*)   You've got lots of teas here . . . where did you buy all this stuff?

Edward   Went to this place in the market, some tea specialist, Phil. Spent an hour with him. Left an expert. Bought the whole range, none caffeine, green, black, Sri Lankan . . . Even coffee beans. Spent about a hundred quid on all the stuff.

Linda *re-enters. Two cups in hand. She puts one on the coffee table.*

Edward   It's always you that drank all that. Should've come earlier, probably better than just . . . in and out . . .

Linda   Best thing for me, pick up the things I needed to.

Edward   Sure, best thing.

Long pause.

Edward   So my friend.

Linda   The school friend . . . yes.

Edward   Solicitor now . . .

Linda   Oh nice . . .

Edward   Grew up together. (*Slight pause.*) Had me thinking. (*Pause.*) You were studying in Ealing, I remember, and it was around the time his dad died. Suicide. And I remember when the funeral was, at the back of Harrow Road, that big Catholic church, and all the boys, we were all there. I'd just met you, and was in the dog house for being late all the time. And we'd planned to meet that evening, and I didn't have the balls to tell you that I wouldn't be able to meet you during your lunch break cos I was stuck at this funeral. Getting from Harrow Road to Ealing Broadway . . . I just stood outside the church, could see his family, all the way inside there, him and . . . And I just stood outside, then kinda just left. Funny the things we do . . .

Pause.

What are you doing tonight? . . . Come even for an hour . . .

Linda   Edward . . .

Edward   I just thought . . .

Linda   Don't . . .

Edward   Fair enough . . . (*Pause.*) Just. (*Slight pause.*) What do I say when I tell them I'm married.

Linda   Separated . . .. My solicitor sent you lots of emails. Your friend, he's a solicitor.

Edward   Criminal law, different thing . . . (*Pause.*) I just haven't had a chance to . . .

Linda   Things you want to split in half . . .

Edward   A lot of other things I'm sorting out . . . Quit my job.

Linda   I know what you're like, don't decorate it.

Edward   OK. I left, yeah . . . They were gonna sack me . . .

Linda   So why lie about it?

Edward   I'm . . . it's not that I am . . .

Linda   Don't wanna get into this.

Edward   With all this, just saying, all the things I'm dealing with, you attack me with the divorce stuff?

Linda   If it feels that way I'm sorry, but Ed . . .

Edward   Yeah . . . I mean whatever . . . whatever you wanna do . . . What can I say?

Long pause.

Linda   What will you do? For work . . .

Edward   I'm writing a novel, finally.

Linda   Is that the best use of your time . . . ? (*Pause.*) No. Sorry. You can do what you want . . . What am I saying.

Edward   Used to it . . . everything I did, always asked you . . .

Linda   Don't have to.

Edward   Some kind of weird seeking of your approval. (*Pause.*) But now, no need. The grass is greener, you know . . . Or it's supposed to be . . . (*Slight pause.*) This stuff . . . Pretend we don't have feelings. Be so fucking business like.

Linda   I hate this house. Hate how it smells.

Long pause.

My parents want to sell. I'm sorry.

Edward   They wrote. You could've told me yourself.

Long pause.

Know what I remember . . . ?

Linda   Yeah?

Edward   My back . . .

Linda   What about it?

Edward   Fucked it painting the skirtings . . .

Linda   Yep.

Edward   DIY king, that was me . . .

Linda   Till we called someone to fix everything you damaged.

Pause.

Edward   Had us some pretty amazing times down here, didn't we?

Linda   A few . . .

Edward   I remember right by that time I had that office . . . for all of six months. And Jess is about a year old . . . always had coffee before I went there . . .

Linda   Spent more time there than you did here . . . Even your birthday . . . Obsessive creative. Didn't come home . . .

Edward   I wanted to . . . (*Pause.*) I'm sorry . . .

Linda   What for? Nothing to be sorry about . . .

Edward   Spending it together . . . I remember . . . We didn't because of . . .

Linda   It was me . . . I thought I'd get a taxi, come up all that way to see you, it was so late. I had so little battery on my phone, and I was there, your light was on, and I knocked . . . and you didn't answer . . . Had Jess in my arms, and I was out there . . . I don't know why I did it. That childish thing in me to surprise you . . . Taking a little baby out with me so late . . . I just thought you'd be so happy to see me, and you were working so hard . . . and I didn't know how to get back home . . . All the way in north London and I didn't know what to do . . .

Edward   I didn't expect you to come. I . . .

Linda   What?

Edward   I was restless, went for a walk, I regret leaving you and Jess out there.

Linda   Your phone was on. I heard it in there ringing. What is wrong with you?

Edward   Nothing.

Linda   Jesus Christ, still making excuses about it . . .

Edward   What should I say? One night. I don't know. Yes, I went for a walk, came back to the office, slept and didn't wake up till midday, saw all the missed calls, the voicemails from you, I was horrified . . . What am I supposed to do? God . . . I know, yes, OK. I let you down, I was so chaotic then.

Linda   . . . I just came to get my things . . .

Edward   Made mistakes.

Linda   . . . And I'm bringing this up . . .

Pause.

You never were seeing another woman, were you?

Edward *remains silent.*

Linda   . . . Don't wanna know . . . I should be going . . .

Linda *puts her coat on, begins picking up her things.*

Jess . . . You should see what she's like, the intonations in her voice, the way her personality is so . . . she's amazing.

Edward   I have to come and see her, Linda; I must do that.

Linda   You have to, she's your daughter.

Edward   I think I should.

Linda   Of course you should. What's wrong with you? What are you talking about?

Edward   Just saying.

Linda   Make it sound like it's just something you have to do at some point in your life.

Edward   I've got it in my plans to . . .

Linda   When?

Edward   What am I supposed to do? Just turn up, kick your door down?

Linda   I never stopped you . . .

Long pause.

She's got her first ballet show. I enrolled her months back
. . . Weston-super-Mare.

Edward   When?

Linda   Couple of weeks . . . (*Going into her bag. Looking for
something.*) I've got my open return ticket . . . from
Paddington, I checked the train you'd have to catch, wrote it
down . . . The date . . .

Edward   Weston, what's it like up there? Isn't that the place
where there's the sea, but no sea . . . ?

Linda (*laughs*)   Yes . . . First week up there . . . kept telling
her, we're going up by the sea . . . My whole childhood,
never went there, maybe once . . . You forget this stuff . . .

Edward   Childhood memories . . .

Linda   It was unusually hot for May. It was so hot in the car
getting down there . . . all this traffic right down to the coast
. . . We finally get there . . . me and Jess, her in her little
bathing suit, these big white armbands on either arm . . . All
day we'd spent getting ready, we were itching to swim in the
water. And I'm there running . . . Picnic bag in hand . . .
She's behind me, this excitement on her face. And I turn
and look out . . . All I see is beach, no water at all . . . It was
an estuary. Suddenly I remembered . . . I didn't even have
the heart to tell her . . . Spent the whole afternoon filling our
bucket with water from the outdoor shower . . . building
sandcastles . . .

Pause.

Sometimes I'm with her . . . She's like you.

Pause.

This melancholy . . . she's quiet.

Pause.

Edward   . . . You've just got this new life, new house . . .

Linda   I had to . . .

Edward   What do you want me to say? It was awful? I know it was. Yes, OK; I begged you to stay but you had to leave, and I don't want to make any excuses but . . .

Linda   I'm sorry . . .

Pause.

Edward   Why would Jess even wanna see me? I look into her eyes, they're so honest . . . they are . . . like these mirrors, I see things about me.

Linda   . . . Hope these glasses don't damaged on the train . . .

Edward   When you left . . . Didn't stop you. The most decent thing I could fucking do . . . Where was I . . . Always writing . . . All I'd ever say, as if, as if ever . . .? I never put a pen on a piece of paper . . . not even to write my name.

Linda   Ed . . .

Edward   I just couldn't get a grip . . . And I tell myself this lie, tell myself all the time, and I remember this one night, I came home, and I had told you I was writing and I wasn't, I was getting so drunk . . . And I stumbled into the house, you and Jess both asleep, and I get into bed, and I knew, I felt it then . . . nothing was better than that feeling, nothing . . . And I just watched you both . . .

Linda   I want you to be there . . . for her . . .

Edward   I just know that if I had that bit of time . . . What I could be . . . (*Slight pause.*) Don't carry all this stuff back with you . . . I'll get a van . . . Let's drive up together . . . Pick up food on the way . . . See Jess . . .

Linda   I'm in a relationship now. (*Slight pause.*) I want to be respectful to that.

Long pause.

We were your family. Your daughter is still your family. Be there for her.

Pause.

It will kill you for the rest of your life, and when she's eighteen and she finds you and wants to know why, why you couldn't just turn up . . . be there . . .

Edward (*after a pause*)   What am I supposed to do?

Linda (*handing* **Edward** *a travel card*)   Here . . . please.

Edward *takes the travel card.*

Linda   Don't wait till she's . . . too old. (*Pause.*) I have to go.

Edward   I'll help you downstairs . . .

Linda   No . . .

Linda *turns to leave. Stops.*

Sometimes I miss you . . . Don't even care about what you've done, things you've hidden. (*Pause.*) I'll call next week.

Linda *leaves.* **Edward** *makes his way back to the sofa. His eyes fixed on the travel card. He looks up at the room around him.*

Slow fade.

Scene Five

Hours later. Night. **Edward** *asleep on the sofa. The flat somewhat neater, some boxes with belongings piled beside him. The door slightly ajar. The door buzzes. Silence. It buzzes again. A silence. Eventually* **Brian**, *noticeably smarter dressed, in clothes that don't suit him at all, enters the flat, remaining by the door. He notices* **Edward** *asleep on the sofa.*

Brian (*whispering*)   Ed? (*He looks around. Louder.*) Hey!
Eddie!

Edward   Huh? What?

Brian   Ed?

Edward (*noticing him*)   Brian? You're here . . .

Brian   The fuck! Of course I'm fucking here, what am I?
Anyone in?

Edward   Just me . . . (*Sitting up.*) Fuck . . . I'm sorry . . .
come in.

Brian   Don't mind if I do, Ed. Don't mind at all, but where
I wanna be is out. Phoned. Nothing. Waited, phoned you
again, thought oh man. Knew you'd do this. Just knew!

Edward   No, I'm . . . Jesus . . . I didn't mean to crash . . .

Brian   My fairy godmother was kind enough to point me to
the spare one hundred and fifty quid I had stashed under
my sofa . . . Pay for this . . . (*Indicating his clothes.*) I'm
supposed to be at the fucking ball right now, for fuck
sake . . .

Edward   What time is it?

Brian   Early hours. Still time to make an entrance . . .

Edward   Sorry . . . I'm . . .

He gets up, tries to stumbles.

Brian   You been at it, ain't you?

Edward   I'm sorry . . . Oh fuck, man . . .

Brian   Some fucking man of your word you are. (*Looking
around.*) What is fucking happening in here? You moving
out? Left the door open . . .

Edward   Just need a minute . . .

Brian (*pacing*) OK, OK, OK . . . it's fucking OK. Been thinking about it . . . good timing . . . We get there now? Good timing . . . We would've got their earlier, think what crap we would've had to sit through . . . some formal five course bollocks . . . having chit chats about nothing over some dirty lobster fucking bisque . . . (*Slight pause.*) OK, we've probably missed the few very appealing single women who by now would be off the market . . . God knows, but at this time, there are a few, I am sure, few locals, still hanging around, looking for a shag, might be a bit older, drink in their hand waiting for us to burst right in there . . . (*Slight pause.*) I admit, I haven't had a drink yet . . . But I want one . . . Bit tense . . . But couldn't . . . I mean . . . I did what you said, our agreement, kept it sober . . . but well, you've gone and fucked that right up. I kept to it.

Edward I went already . . . sorry.

Pause.

Brian What a fucking horrible thing to do.

Edward No . . . I didn't go inside . . . didn't . . . Stood across the street . . .

Brian Doing what? Being a fucking voyeur? A perv?

Edward Not like that . . .

Brian The fuck, no way we can go there now, is there? That's fucking selfish . . .

Edward I'm sorry . . .

Brian Fucking waste of my money, not gonna wear what I'm wearing again, am I. Bought it for this . . . Dressed like a done up turkey for fuck all . . .

Edward I stood there and I wanted to just see.

Brian Yeah, you and me both . . .

Edward   Wanted to see what it was like. This town house, three floors, all theirs. Gravel, gate, you name it, large windows . . . all of them inside . . .

Slight pause.

Brian   Fuck it . . . probably wasn't worth it anyway.

Edward   . . . I wish that was my house.

Brian   Yeah. You don't say.

Pause.

Brian   If you still wanna go . . .

Edward   Nah . . .

Brian   Yeah, nah. (*Slight pause.*) . . . Random thought, innit . . . (*Slight pause.*) Bit of eye candy . . . admire the wallpaper, talk about the wallpaper with a few stragglers.

Edward   Thing about tonight . . . thing about it . . .?

Brian   Yeah . . .?

Edward   We won't find what we're looking for.

Brian   Bought a pack of condoms.

Edward   Yeah, well . . .

Pause.

Sorry.

Brian   If you're sorry, as you say . . . We could . . .

Edward   For everything.

Brian   Cos, there's me . . . holding out for a fucking drink for how long . . .?

Slight pause.

Edward   I never liked you . . .

Brian   Yeah. Never liked you neither . . .

Edward   In fact, I fucking hate you . . . No way would I have taken you with me.

Brian   What you fucking on about now?

Edward   I'm telling you. Coming to your house, after school . . . Fourteen. I'd walk in and your mum looked like she was about to burst into tears if I spoke, and your dad, storming out, like he'd just threatened to smack the shit out of her.

Brian   Yeah . . . That's about right, so fucking what?

Edward   All I remember about you. (*Slight pause.*) I liked seeing it . . . being there cos the longer I stayed the more I couldn't wait to go home, see my parents. Them there putting dinner out, or listening to the radio, or reading, some newspaper, TV . . . Eating together, planning the next family holiday . . . Only reason I came over . . . Only reason I hung around with you . . . Use you to remind myself how fucking normal I was . . . not some fucked up cunt! Always knew you'd turn out fucked up. Just had to see it for myself.

Brian *calmly walks over to* **Edward**. *Stands over him.*

Brian   Go on, get up . . .

Edward *stands up.*

Edward   Smack me, go on . . . You fuck up! You dickhead. Go on. See how hard you can . . .

Brian *smacks* **Edward** *flush in the face. He falls knocking over the pile of boxes behind him.*

Brian   Want some more?

Brian *watches* **Edward** *who remains on the floor. Pause.* **Brian** *checks his wrist, heads to the table, pours himself a drink, knocks it back.* **Brian** *pours himself another. Drinks it again, in one. He heads for the door.*

Edward   Hang about for a bit . . .

Brian *stops.*

Edward   Please . . .

Pause. **Brian** *continues to watch him.*

Edward   I've been lying. (*Pause.*) She ain't coming back . . . She ain't. . . (*Pause.*) She left April.

Long pause.

Ain't seen my daughter since neither . . .

Pause.

Brian   Only free advice I'm giving you . . . You on the birth certificate, all that . . .? Go file an application at court. Cost you two hundred and fifty quid. . . You selfish cunt.

Edward   Don't wanna see her.

Brian   Why?

Edward   Don't wanna see Linda, don't wanna see my daughter neither . . . fuck 'em . . . both of 'em.

Brian   Your daughter, not mine. Your funeral.

Edward   What do they care? Tell me . . . They don't give a fuck . . . One thing about me . . . I know, I have my failings. Fuck me, I do. But when you're low . . . Head on the fucking ground, can't get up . . . they jump ship . . .

Pause.

Came here today . . . collected her things. Her parents . . . Selling up this place.

Brian   Don't worry, shit always gets better.

Edward   She's got a new partner now . . .

Brian   OK. Shit will get better. But eventually.

Pause.

Edward Before you came . . . was here, thinking about
what I used to do when I used to come to your place . . . As a
kid. My own place. That functional family set up I thought I
had . . . I think about it . . . Don't know how they did it . . .

Brian Did what?

Edward Hide it from us, you know . . . Flat out fucking
pretend . . . (*Slight pause.*) As a kid you look at your parents,
like they're gonna be together forever and that's how it is . . .
But it's just this fucking show they're putting on for your
benefit . . . (*Pause.*) And you get to that age, and you're
trying to do things like them . . . bring in money . . . Be some
shoulder to cry on . . . Always give love whatever happens
. . . Like as if marriage is some fucking instinctive thing,
when it's . . . (*Pause.*) It isn't . . . (*Pause.*) Hard . . . (*Pause.*)
Trying to be better . . . Trying . . .

Long pause.

I remember . . . (*Pause.*) Was seeing this girl, I knew it was
wrong, always ate me up . . . And I broke it off . . . things
were so bad, I had to . . . (*Pause.*) I'm there in the school . . .
lunch, where we worked . . . told her, wanted nothing to do
with her. Nothing . . . For once . . . Do the right fucking
thing . . . (*Slight pause.*) Soon as I tell her . . . She slaps me, I
pushed her back . . . Get her away from me . . . Next thing I
know, someone's got me in a headlock, my nose bleeding . . .
Throwing me out of the front entrance, in front of all these
students . . . Didn't even care . . . didn't even wait for them
to sack me . . . Fuck it . . . Just wanted to fix things with
Linda. Just wanted to be at home . . . I knew what I was
doing this for . . . I knew . . . Just knew if I could go there, to
her, give love, it would break through the months of us not
talking, months of not coming home . . . (*Slight pause.*) And I
get home, it's not even the afternoon, still the morning . . . I
tell her I took the day off . . . I put everything in the car, my
daughter in her car seat. Tell them we're going to the Isle of
Wight . . . A few days . . . just us . . . (*Slight pause.*) I knew if I
could just get them there with me, some place away from all

the shit . . . All the things I wanted to say, how much I
needed them, and loved them . . . It'd just come out of me
. . . (*Pause.*) Instead, the whole way there, bickering, couldn't
even get past Southampton . . . Parked in the car park
screaming at each other till it was dark . . . The amount of
hate between us . . . And I knew . . . I knew if I didn't do
something, knew. Knew her dad was gonna be on his way
down to us. I had about three hours . . . time it took from
Wales . . . Knew I just had to say the truth . . . That I was
fucking stupid and scared, not fucking good enough,
controlling . . . I didn't wanna be . . . That I was in a dark
place and I needed her to just help me . . . just a bit . . . And
I'm trying to say this . . . But what comes out of me are
words that cut into her, her eyes red, full of anger and hurt,
and suddenly I look, see the pain I'm causing, see that if I
could just be brave enough to just pull her close, she
would've understood . . . (*Slight pause.*) And just as I'm about
to . . . Her dad gets there . . . laying into me about having to
bomb it though Winchester A-roads, hundred miles an hour
to protect his daughter and all this bollocks . . . About me
being responsible for all the speeding tickets he'll get.
(*Pause.*) And she's looking at me. And I'm doing nothing.
Saying nothing. Letting them get in the car . . . Watching
them go . . . (*Pause.*) I knew that was it . . .

A silence.

Said I'd go up there . . . See her you know . . . Some ballet
show she's got. My daughter . . .

Brian   When?

Edward   Couple weeks . . . dunno.

Long pause.

Brian   Go with you if you need . . . Least I could do . . . Feel
like such a cunt laying you out . . . Coming here smacking
you . . .

Edward   No, I deserve it . . .

Brian   No . . . Dropped my standards . . . I'm ashamed . . . You're homeless . . . I shouldn't've. . .

Pause.

Edward   Don't think I can stay here . . .

Pause.

Brian   Can stay at mine . . . If you want . . .

Edward   Europop is not what I need right now . . .

Brian   . . . Yeah.

Edward   But I can't stay here . . .

Brian   Nah . . .

Slight pause.

Edward   . . . The fucking lies.

Brian   Yeah . . .

Edward   Lies to myself. . .

Brian   Too fucking many . . .

Edward (*to himself*)   How do they do it . . .?

Brian   Pathetic . . . World full of self-advertising, lying wankers . . .

Edward   Exactly . . .

Brian   Exactly.

Pause.

Edward   I mean, you're honest . . . say the truth about shit . . . ? How you fucking feel . . .

Brian   Who can handle it? Think you're crazy   . . . Eats you up . . .

Pause.

Edward   That's why we've gotta go . . .

Brian   Yeah . . . Where . . .?

Edward   Hampstead . . .

Brian   Yeah . . .?

Edward   Yeah . . . Bap-fucking-tiste . . .

Brian   What we're doing . . .?

Edward   Yes.

Brian (*smartening himself*)   Talk about the wallpaper . . .
Works every time.

Edward   No, Brian. Fuck that! Fuck the small talk . . .

Brian   OK. Fuck small talk . . . Yes.

Edward   Fuck you, Baptiste . . . We're here! Crashing the
fuck in!

Brian   Yes! . . .

Edward   'Real life' has arrived . . . For fuck.

Brian   Yes . . . For fuck . . .

Long pause. **Brian** *watches* **Edward**.

Brian   Meet me downstairs . . . ?

Pause.

Edward   Meet you downstairs.

Brian *exits, returns, takes the bottle of vodka from the table, exits.*
Edward *slowly grabs hold of his keys, small things. Knocks into one
of the boxes, picks it up, putting it back on the pile neatly. Heads to
the door. Turns to look into the room. Turns the light off shutting the
door.*

THE END

www.ingramcontent.com/pod-product-compliance
Ingram Content Group UK Ltd.
Pitfield, Milton Keynes, MK11 3LW, UK
UKHW020708280225
455688UK00012B/319